make it in
**Minutes**

# Mini-Books

# Mini-Books

## ROXI PHILLIPS

A Division of Sterling Publishing Co., Inc., New York

**Book Editor**

Lecia Monsen

**Copy Editors**

Lisa Anderson

Catherine Risling

**Photographer**

Zachary Williams
Williams Visual
Ogden, UT

**Photo Stylist**

Annie Hampton

**Book Designer**

Kehoe + Kehoe Design
Associates, Inc.
Burlington, VT

*Other Books
in this Series:*

Make It in Minutes:
Greeting Cards

Make It in Minutes:
Beaded Jewelry

Make It in Minutes:
Mini-Boxes

Make It in Minutes:
Party Favors
& Hostess Gifts

**A Red Lips 4 Courage Communications, Inc. book**
www.redlips4courage.com
Eileen Cannon Paulin
*President*
Catherine Risling
*Editorial Director*

10 9 8 7 6 5 4 3 2 1

First Edition

Published by Lark Books, A Division of
Sterling Publishing Co., Inc.
387 Park Avenue South, New York, N.Y. 10016

Text © 2007, Roxi Phillips
Photography © 2007, Lark Books
Illustrations © 2007, Lark Books

Distributed in Canada by Sterling Publishing,
c/o Canadian Manda Group, 165 Dufferin Street
Toronto, Ontario, Canada M6K 3H6

Distributed in the United Kingdom by GMC Distribution Services,
Castle Place, 166 High Street, Lewes, East Sussex, England BN7 1XU

Distributed in Australia by Capricorn Link (Australia) Pty Ltd.,
P.O. Box 704, Windsor, NSW 2756 Australia

If you have questions or comments about this book, please contact:
Lark Books
67 Broadway
Asheville, NC 28801
(828) 253-0467
Manufactured in China
All rights reserved

ISBN 13: 978-1-60059-034-4
ISBN 10: 1-60059-034-9

For information about custom editions, special sales, premium and corporate
purchases, please contact Sterling Special Sales Department at (800) 805-5489;
or e-mail specialsales@sterlingpub.com.

"Books are humanity in print."

—Barbara W. Tuchman

Contents

planning A birthday

# Introduction

Everyone enjoys photo albums and scrapbooks, yet there is something charming about mini-books. They beg you to hold them in your hands, note every element, pull every tag, and read every word.

Mini-books come in all shapes, colors, and styles and provide a special place to gather thoughts and memories. They can evoke a feeling, document a special time, or provide a snapshot into the everyday happenings of life. In one of these little gems, even the simplest topic is given importance. After all, isn't it really the simple things in life that bring us the most pleasure?

In this book you will find a treasure trove of miniature albums created using basic techniques and a handful of materials in a variety of themes. They can be created in minutes and then you can spend as much time as you wish embellishing the pages to make them uniquely your own. Perhaps it's true that the best things in life really do come in small packages.

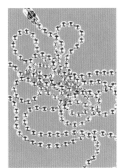

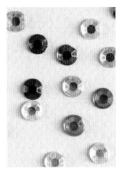

# CHAPTER 1

I think it is exciting to begin the creative process. Sometimes my ideas come from the most unusual places like a song lyric, billboard, or quote. Design compositions, color themes, and ideas are everywhere if your mind is open. When beginning a mini-book, consider the story you want to tell or the purpose the book will serve. Think about the feeling you want to portray and the colors, papers, and embellishments that will best accomplish that goal. Begin by gathering the materials, tools, photographs, memorabilia, and basic supplies. Familiarize yourself with the simple techniques and the list of tools contained in this chapter and you will be well on your way to creating amazing projects in very little time.

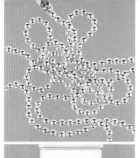

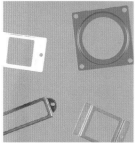

# Embellishments

### Ball chains
Ball chains and fasteners have traditionally been used as lamp pulls and key chains but have found a new role as unique mini-book bindings. The chains and connectors can be purchased in an array of colors and lengths. Cut the chain between the linked balls using wire cutters or old scissors. Thread the chain through a hole in the book's spine and insert the last ball on the chain into the connector and pull into place, creating a loop.

### Bookbinding tape
Usually self-adhesive, bookbinding tape is available in a variety of colors and widths. It works well to rein-force bindings and to strengthen folds on paper and chipboard. Bookbinding tape also makes an interest-ing embellishment behind titles or as a background layer, and readily accepts ink to coordinate with other elements in a project.

### Bookplates
Bookplates are label holders attached to a project with a brad on either side. A paper label is inserted into the top of the plate.

### Brads
Brads come in many colors, sizes, and shapes and can be used to hold elements in place or as decora-tion on their own. They are simply pushed through paper using a small, pre-punched hole; the prongs are then spread open and flattened on the back to secure.

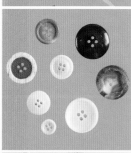

### Buttons
Buttons can add a sense of whimsy or an elegant appeal. Adhere to projects with craft glue or glue dots or string several on wire or thread to create a dimensional accent.

### Charms
There are charms for practically every theme imaginable. Dangle them from ribbons or fibers or adhere them with metal embellishment adhesive or glue dots.

### Chipboard cut-outs
Shapes of every sort, including alphabet letters, add an exciting dimension to a design. Cutouts can be painted, sanded, or covered with paper.

### Craft wire
This versatile product, available in a wide variety of colors and gauges, can be used to string beads, create spirals, or bind a mini-book. Adhere to projects with glue dots.

### Die cuts
Typically made of cardstock or paper, an enormous array is available to add the perfect touch to a paper craft project. Make-it-yourself die cuts, in a range of prices, are available as well.

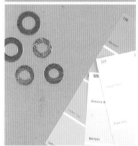

### Hardware
The aisles of a hardware store yield a variety of materials useful in creating paper projects, such as screen material, washers, paint chips, and fasteners. Most require metal embellishment adhesive or double-sided tape to support their weight.

### Jewels and sequins
Add glamour and sparkle to your pages with these little gems. Adhere to projects with craft glue or glue dots.

### Office supplies
Paper clips, safety pins, file tabs, shipping labels, and other office supplies are well suited for use in embellishing books.

## Timely Thoughts
Keep a journal or notebook close by to record special thoughts and treasured moments with your loved ones. You will be a step ahead when it's time to create a special gift.

### Paper flowers
Paper flowers add dimension and interest. Adhere using glue dots or craft glue. For an additional accent, punch a small hole in the middle of a flat flower and insert a decorative brad or an eyelet to mimic the center.

### Photo corners
Designed to hold a photo in place on a page, many photo corners are self-adhesive. They are available in many colors and sizes.

### Ribbon
Use ribbon as embellishments to bind a book, knot onto tags, or adhere directly onto a page with glue dots or craft glue.

### Rub-ons
These adhesive decals are applied to the surface of a project using a craft stick. Available in numerous colors, images, fonts, and styles, rub-ons are a wonderful way to add a decorative touch.

### Slide mounts
Originally used for photographic slides, these frames come in many sizes and materials such as plastic, paper, and metal. Use them to frame quotes, titles, memorabilia, or photos. Adhere with glue dots or double-sided tape.

### Stapler and staples
Decorative staples are used with a stapler designed specifically for their size. Regular staples can be colored with permanent markers.

## time-saving tip
## Ready-Made, Set, Go!
To save time and steps, purchase a ready-made embellishment for a book's cover or pages.

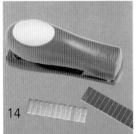

# Adhesives

**Adhesive dispenser**

**Craft glue**

**Double-sided tape**

**Foam mounting dots**

**Foam mounting tape**

**Glue dots**

**Glue stick**

**Hot glue sticks**

**Vellum tape**

# Additional Supplies

There are many everyday items that will help you craft and decorate miniature books. Some are as simple as a ruler, stapler, and pencils, while others are a bit less common. A bone folder, for example, is typically shaped like a letter opener and is essential in achieving a clean fold in paper and cardstock.

- Computer and printer
- Cosmetic sponges
- Craft knife
- Craft scissors
- Journaling pens
- Metal-edge ruler
- Paper trimmer
- Pencils
- Sandpaper

# Tools

**Decorative-edge scissors**

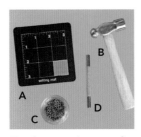

**Eyelet-setting tools**
A Setting mat   C Eyelets
B Craft hammer  D Eyelet setter

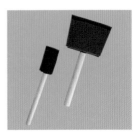

**Foam brushes**

**Hole punch**

**Inkpad**

**Label maker**

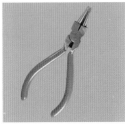

**Needle-nose pliers**

**Paper punch**

**Piercing tool**

**Rubber stamps**

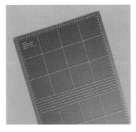

**Self-healing cutting mat**

**Wire cutters**

# Techniques

## Accordion folding

Cut paper to desired size and then use a metal-edge ruler to measure and mark equal increments on the top and bottom edges of the strip. Line the ruler up on each set of marks and draw a line with a scoring tool from top to bottom. You may need to go over the line a few times if you are working with thick cardstock or paper. Fold each scored line in the opposite direction as the previous scored line, like a fan. The folds that point down are referred to as valley folds and the folds that point up are mountain folds. Scoring boards, available on the market, easily make accurate scored lines.

## Applying rub-ons

Rub-ons come on a transfer sheet and often contain several images. Carefully cut out the chosen image. Position on the project and firmly rub the image with a craft stick or rub-on tool until it is completely transferred. Do not lift the backing paper off until you are sure you have a successful transfer. When rubbing images, avoid pushing too hard or it will cause cracks in the image.

## Covering chipboard and mitering corners

Apply a thin layer of craft glue to one side of the chipboard piece using a foam brush. Place chipboard, glue side down, onto back side of decorative paper. Trim paper diagonally across all of the corners just outside of the chipboard piece. *Note:* The distance of the cut from the chipboard corners should be equal to the thickness of the chipboard. Fold and adhere paper onto the back side of the chipboard; allow to dry.

## Heat embossing

Stamp an image with embossing or pigment ink and then cover with embossing powder; tap off excess. Use a heat tool to melt the powder; allow to cool.

## Inking

Simply tap a permanent inkpad around the edge of a paper or photograph for a distressed, framed effect. For a softer look, apply ink by patting a cosmetic sponge onto the inkpad and then dab it lightly onto the edges or surface of the elements.

## Matting photos

Cut a piece of coordinating cardstock or scrapbook paper ⅛"–¼" larger than the photo. Center and adhere it onto the back of the image with double-sided tape or an adhesive dispenser. For additional flair, trim the edges of the mat with decorative-edge scissors before adhering the photo.

## Printing on scrapbook paper

To print on scrapbook paper, use 8½"x11" pages or cut larger sheets down to that size and print as usual.

## Rubber stamping

For the best effect, pat the stamp on the inkpad several times. Press firmly onto the desired surface. Lift off carefully without smearing ink. *Note:* Dye ink typically dries quickly while pigment ink may take some time. To speed drying time, set pigment ink with a heat tool.

## Setting eyelets

To set an eyelet, punch a small hole in the paper with a piercing tool or hole punch where the eyelet is to be set. Insert eyelet through hole and position project face down on a craft mat. Using setting tool and hammer on a setting mat, flatten the eyelet's prongs and secure in place. *Note:* Some eyelet setters don't require a hammer; simply follow the manufacturer's instructions.

## Silhouetting photographed images

Carefully cut just outside the edge of desired image using sharp, pointed-tip scissors. Avoid cutting too close to the image, especially faces and hair. *Note:* This requires some practice, so cut out a photocopy of the image first.

## Tearing paper

Holding the edge of desired paper, with a hand on either side of the area to be torn, pull one hand towards yourself. To tear a straight line, paint a line of water to weaken the paper where you want it to tear. *Note:* This is especially effective with mulberry and natural fiber papers. Most paper has a grain and will tear better in one direction than the other.

# Stab Binding

## Materials

- Book
- Craft scissors
- Heavy-duty hole punch
- Pencil
- Ruler
- Waxed thread

## Instructions

1. Mark and punch two holes on binding of book ½" from edge and evenly spaced from top and bottom edges. *Note:* If you don't have a heavy-duty hole punch, take the book to a copy shop and have the holes drilled.

2. Cut waxed thread to equal approximately four times length of book spine; thread through needle.

3. Working on bottom hole, guide waxed thread through hole from front to back, leaving 4" tail in front (A).

4. Loop around bottom of binding and back through bottom hole (B).

5. From back, loop around left edge of binding and back down through bottom hole (C) and then up through top hole.

6. Repeat Steps 3–5 for top hole.

7. Tighten tails and knot on center front of book; trim as desired.

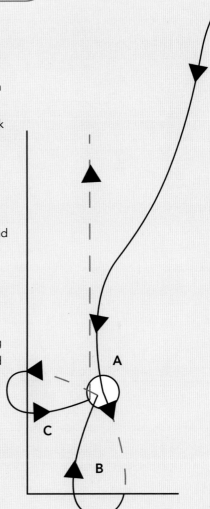

## CHAPTER 2

In this day and age, when everyone is busy and families are often pulled in many directions, I believe it is important that we spend time playing, vacationing, and keeping traditions alive. By being together we create fond memories and form bonds worthy of documenting in special ways. Miniature books dedicated to the times we share allow us to hold onto our family experiences and pass them down from one generation to the next. With a handful of pictures, some carefully chosen papers and embellishments, and a few simple techniques, you will be able to preserve important moments in the lives of your loved ones. In this chapter you will find projects that will inspire you to take those special moments and transform them into treasured keepsakes.

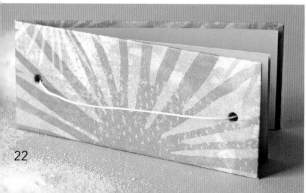

# Seashore Memories

## Materials

- Acid-free adhesive dispenser
- Beads: small (6)
- Cardstock: coordinating colors
- Chipboard
- Craft scissors
- Hole punch: 3/16"
- Inkpads: coordinating colors (2–3)
- Rubber stamps: tropical-themed
- Scrapbook paper: tropical-themed
- Thread: heavyweight off-white (16")

## Instructions

1. **To create covers:** Cut two 2"x 5" pieces of chipboard and two 4"x 7" pieces of scrapbook paper. Cover chipboard with paper, mitering corners to back side of covers; adhere with adhesive dispenser.

2. Cut two 1½"x 3¾" pieces of cardstock; adhere to mitered sides of covers. Punch holes in covers, ½" in from narrow ends and 1" from top. Embellish front cover as desired.

3. **To create pages:** Cut five 4¾"x 1⅞" pieces of cardstock. Mark and punch holes using cover as a template. Stamp tropical images onto pages; embellish as desired.

4. **To assemble book:** Layer covers and pages as desired. Knot one end of thread 4" from end; thread unknotted end down through left hole, along back cover, and up through right hole. Knot 4" from end. String three beads onto each end of thread and knot to secure; trim excess close to knots.

## time-saving tip

### Easy, Breezy Backgrounds

Make custom backgrounds on the pages faster and easier by stamping images onto a full piece of cardstock before cutting it into pages.

# Cousins by the Dozens

## Materials

- Acid-free adhesives: $\frac{1}{8}$" tacky tape, dispenser, double-sided tape
- Cardstock: coordinating (2); off-white (1)
- Chipboard
- Craft scissors
- Fiber: yarn (2')
- Label maker and label tape
- Letters: chipboard monograms
- Paper punch: corner rounder
- Scoring tool
- Scrapbook paper: coordinating colors and patterns (2)
- Spray paint: black

## Instructions

1. **To create back cover:** Cut one 6"x 5¼" piece of chipboard and one 8"x 7¼" piece of scrapbook paper. Cover chipboard with paper, mitering corners to back side; adhere using adhesive dispenser.

2. **To create front cover:** Cut two 3"x 5¼" pieces of chipboard and two 5"x 7¼" pieces of scrapbook paper. Cover chipboard pieces with scrapbook paper, mitering corners to back side of covers; adhere using adhesive dispenser.

3. **To create accordion binding:** Cut two 4"x 5¼" pieces of coordinating cardstock. Score and fold at ½" increments across 4" width, starting and ending with valley folds. Adhere one accordion fold onto each back cover side using double-sided tape. *Note:* Be sure to line up the first fold of the accordion spine with the edge of the back cover.

4. Adhere each remaining end of accordion onto corresponding edges of front covers. Adhere outside accordion folds together using tacky tape in creases.

## time-saving tip

### Adding Pages
**Increase the number of pages in a gatefold mini-book by extending the length of the cardstock binding and folding extra accordion pleats to accommodate the additional pages.**

**Top:** The staggered pages provide a striking format for showing a chronological progression of stages or events. **Above:** Staggered pages open up to reveal a perfect spot for journaling.

5. Cut two 2¾"x 5" pieces of scrapbook paper; adhere on inside front covers over accordion edge with double-sided tape. Cut one 5"x 5¾" piece of scrapbook paper; adhere onto inside back cover with double-sided tape. Print journaling on off-white cardstock; trim and adhere onto inside back cover.

6. **To create pages:** Cut six 4½"x 2½" pieces of cardstock; round corners of one end with paper punch. Adhere squared end on top edge of left accordion. Position two additional tags on remaining two flaps 1" lower than previous tag. Repeat with remaining tags on right-side accordion beginning ⅝" below top and spacing 1" lower for each subsequent tag and flap.

7. Cut one 4¾"x 5½" piece of scrapbook paper; mat with cardstock. Cut in half across 5½" width; adhere each piece onto covers lined up exactly with book opening.

**Above:** Adhering the outside folds of an accordion creates a sturdy bookbinding that will hold pages neatly in place.

8. **To embellish front covers:** Spray chipboard letters with black spray paint; allow to dry. Tie yarn on letter; adhere letters onto book front covers slightly overlapping opening on each side. Create remainder of title words with label maker and mat with cardstock; adhere to cover. Embellish pages as desired.

## time-saving tip

## Page Options

Use ready-made shipping labels or coin envelopes in place of cardstock pages for a quick change of pace. Using envelopes will allow you to include additional memorabilia in your mini-book.

Dedicated to the
**McCaskill
Family**

*Other things may
change, but we
start and end with
family*

FAMILY
*reunion*

# Family Reunion

## Materials

- Acid-free adhesive dispenser
- Cardstock: coordinating color
- Craft scissors
- Ribbon: ¼" gingham
- Scoring tool
- Scrapbook paper: double-sided

## Instructions

1. **To create cover:** Cut one 6"x 12" piece of cardstock. Score and fold in half to form 6" square.

2. **To create pages:** Cut four 6"x 11½" pieces of double-sided scrapbook paper. Stack double-sided papers, alternating patterns. Score and fold in half to form 5¾" square pages.

3. **To assemble book:** Assemble cover and pages in desired order. Trim folded corners at 45-degree angle toward fold, creating tag shape. *Note:* It may be easier to trim the cover first and use it as a template to cut each set of pages.

4. Cut ribbon to 18". Wrap around book and tie in bow on outside of spine.

5. Embellish cover and pages as desired.

# Traveling Sisters

## Materials

- Acid-free adhesive: glue stick
- Beaded fringe
- Cardstock: black
- Chipboard
- Hole punch: $\frac{1}{8}$"
- Pencil
- Ribbon: $\frac{1}{4}$" black, black-and-white checkered
- Scissors: craft, deckle-edge
- Scrapbook paper: dark red

## Instructions

1. **To create covers:** Cut two 5"x 6½" pieces of chipboard. Mark center on short side of one rectangle; cut diagonally to each opposite corner, creating triangle. Repeat with second chipboard piece.

2. **To create pages:** Cut two pieces of scrapbook paper 1" larger than chipboard triangles. Center and adhere paper onto triangles with glue stick, mitering corners onto back side of covers.

3. **To create binding:** Mark placement for three holes ½" in from left edge of cover at 1", 2½", and 4" from top; punch holes. Repeat with remaining cover and pages using front cover as a template.

4. Cut ribbons into 6" lengths; thread one checkered ribbon and one black ribbon through each hole. Knot ribbons loosely. Glue beaded fringe to inside of back cover; allow to dry.

5. Embellish covers and pages as desired.

## time-saving tip

### Beaded Bits

Purchase beaded fringe for a quick and easy embellishment that is sure to impress the lucky recipient.

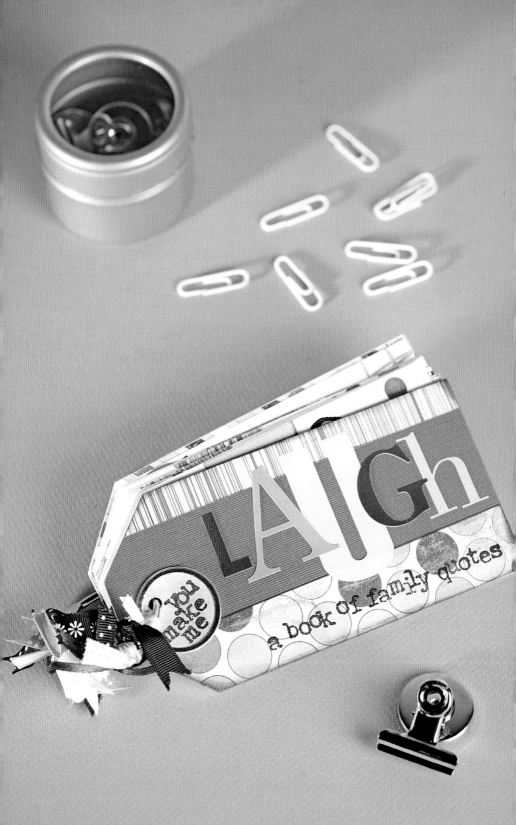

# You Make Me Laugh

## Materials

- Acid-free adhesive dispenser
- Binder ring: $1\frac{1}{2}$"
- Cardstock: navy blue (1), white (2)
- Chipboard
- Cosmetic sponges
- Craft scissors
- Hole punch: $\frac{1}{4}$"
- Inkpads: black, blue, coordinating colors (3)
- Ribbon scraps: coordinating colors (10–12)
- Rubber stamps: small alphabet
- Sanding block
- Scrapbook paper: double-sided coordinating colors and patterns
- Stickers: large letters, coordinating colors
- Tag: $1\frac{1}{4}$" metal-rimmed circle

## Instructions

1. **To create covers:** Cut two 6"x 3" rectangles from chipboard. Trim two corners from one end to make tag shape. Holding tag horizontally with trimmed edge on left, punch $\frac{1}{4}$" hole $\frac{1}{2}$" in from left side.

2. Cut two 6"x 3" rectangles from navy blue cardstock; adhere to one side of each chipboard piece.

3. Cut two 6"x 3" rectangles from scrapbook paper; adhere to remaining sides of chipboard pieces. Sand away extra paper around edges using sanding block.

4. **To embellish cover:** Ink edges of strips of paper with coordinating inkpads and cosmetic sponges; adhere onto front cover.

5. Lightly ink face of metal-rimmed tag with blue ink. Stamp "you make me" in black and adhere tag to cover.

## time-saving tip

### Notable Quotes

**Store this book, along with a few embellished pages, in an easily accessible place so that you can add a new quote whenever you're inspired.**

**Above:** Using giant punctuation marks randomly as embellishments adds a bit of whimsy. **Opposite:** Spare pieces of decorative ribbon tied to the binder ring add color and texture to this delightful tag book.

6. Stamp "a book of family quotes" in black at bottom of front cover. Spell "laugh" with colored letter stickers.

7. **To create pages:** Cut eight 6" x 3" pieces of white cardstock. Trim corners and punch holes in cardstock pieces using chipboard cover as template.

8. **To assemble book:** Layer covers, metal-rimmed tag, and pages on binder ring in desired order. Knot 4" lengths of ribbon on binder ring. Embellish pages as desired.

## time-saving tip

### Double-Takes

**Use coordinating double-sided scrapbook papers to give pages an instant design that requires minimal time and embellishment.**

# Games People Play

## Materials

- Acid-free adhesives: dispenser, glue stick
- Cardstock: off-white
- Chipboard
- Craft scissors
- Scoring tool
- Scrapbook paper: coordinating prints (2)

## Instructions

1. **To create covers:** Cut two 4¾"x 7" pieces of chipboard and two 6¾"x 9" pieces of scrapbook paper. Cover chipboard with paper, mitering corners and adhering onto back side of covers using glue stick.

2. **To create accordion:** Cut two 6½"x 12" pieces of cardstock; score at 4½" increments and fold, making first and last valley folds. *Note:* The last panel on each piece will be 3" long. Overlap 3" panels to create one 4½" panel; adhere with adhesive dispenser.

3. Attach accordion end panels to back sides of covered chipboard using glue stick.

4. Embellish covers and pages as desired.

# A Family Excursion

## Materials

- Acid-free adhesives: craft glue, dispenser
- Acrylic paint
- Cardstock: coordinating colors
- CD pocket sleeves: 5" square (2)
- Chipboard letters
- Cosmetic sponge
- Craft scissors
- Eyelet setting tools
- Eyelets: $\frac{1}{4}$" (4)
- File tabs: self-adhesive (2)
- Foam brush
- Inkpad: brown
- Photos: $3\frac{3}{4}$" square (8)
- Ribbon: $\frac{5}{8}$" (12")
- Rub-ons: alphabet letters
- Sanding block
- Scoring tool
- Scrapbook paper: coordinating colors and patterns
- Tags: $4\frac{3}{4}$"x $2\frac{3}{8}$" (2)

## Instructions

1. **To create covers:** Cut four 5" squares of scrapbook paper; ink edges using inkpad and cosmetic sponge. Adhere one square onto each side of CD sleeve; repeat with remaining sleeve. Stack sleeves so openings are facing each other on right side.

2. Lightly ink two tags. Adhere one tag to center of left side of top CD sleeve, leaving $1\frac{1}{2}$" extending past edge; wrap excess and adhere onto back sleeve. Repeat with remaining tag and back sleeve, overlapping tags to create a hinge.

3. Paint chipboard letters with acrylic paint and foam brush; allow to dry. Adhere letters onto front cover with craft glue and embellish with other items as desired.

## time-saving tip

### Cut & Go
Save yourself a step by printing journaling onto scrapbook papers before cutting them to size and adhering the squares to the inside of the sleeves.

**Top:** CD sleeves create pockets perfect for holding special photos. Just add a title and a few embellishments. **Above:** Vacation snapshots and a bit of journaling tell the story of a special family adventure. **Opposite:** A quote adds just the right finishing touch to the back of this mini-book.

4. **To create binding:** Set two eyelets 1½" from top and bottom in sleeve openings on top of front cover and back cover. Thread ribbon through each eyelet, creating loop; knot to secure and trim excess.

5. **To create accordion:** Cut four 4"x 12" pieces of cardstock; score and fold at 4" increments. Overlap and adhere last panel of one accordion onto first panel of second strip; cut off last panel. Repeat with remaining cardstock strips, creating two accordions with four sections each. Attach file tab to end of each accordion; place folded accordions in sleeves.

6. Sand and ink edges of photos; adhere to each section of accordion. Embellish inner sleeves and accordion strips as desired.

# time-saving tip

## Edge Options
**Use a coordinating color to cover the cut edges of paper and photos. You can even color the edges with a felt-tip pen.**

# Military Family Men

## Materials

- Acid-free adhesives: double-sided tape, glue stick
- Cardstock: black
- Chipboard
- Circle templates: 2¾", 3", 4"
- Craft scissors
- Pencil
- Scoring tool
- Scrapbook paper: theme-related

## Instructions

1. **To create covers:** Cut two 3" circles from chipboard and two 4" circles from scrapbook paper. Center and adhere scrapbook paper onto chipboard circles using glue stick. Snip excess paper in ¼" increments; adhere onto back side of covers.

2. **To create accordion:** Cut two 3" x 11" strips of cardstock; score every 2¾" and fold to create two accordions.

3. Trace 2¾" circle on top panel of one folded accordion. Mark ¾" width on center of both folded edges. Cut out circle accordion, making sure to leave the ¾" widths intact. *Note:* The uncut widths will be the connection between each panel of the accordion, similar to a paper doll chain. Repeat with second accordion.

4. Adhere end circles of each folded strip together using double-sided tape, forming one long accordion. Adhere end of one circle onto back side of cover; repeat with other end and cover.

5. Embellish covers and pages as desired.

## time-saving tip

### Smooth Curves

**After covering a chipboard jacket, roll its edges on a hard surface to smooth out any corners or rough edges.**

## CHAPTER 3

Children grow up all too fast. We wake up one day only to realize our babies have grown up in the blink of an eye. It's easy to forget those first words, tender glances, precious smiles, and dimply knees. By capturing their memorable moments and milestones in small books, we can hold onto those fleeting years more tightly. Whether you're announcing a child's arrival, documenting an event, or recording your wishes for their lives, you'll find inspiration in the projects throughout this chapter. During every childhood there are celebrations and precious moments worthy of being remembered and honored in this unique way. Children will know how treasured they are when they appear as the stars in their very own special books.

# Celebrating Childhood

# Brag Book

## Materials

- Acid-free adhesive dispenser
- Baseball card protectors: heavy-gauge (8)
- Binder ring
- Chalk ink: coordinating color
- Cosmetic sponge
- Craft scissors
- Embellishments: die-cuts, flat buttons, labels, paper clips
- Hole punch: $\frac{1}{4}$"
- Matted photos (8)
- Ribbon: 1" grosgrain coordinating color (24")
- Scrapbook paper: double-sided coordinating colors and patterns

## Instructions

1. **To create pages:** Cut eight $2\frac{5}{8}$"x $3\frac{3}{4}$" pieces of double-sided paper.

2. Embellish paper pieces on both sides using matted photos, flat embellishments, paper clips, and die-cuts; ink edges with cosmetic sponge.

3. Carefully insert completed cards into baseball card protectors.

4. **To assemble book:** Punch hole in upper left corner of each card protector using hole punch; thread cards onto binder ring.

5. Tie four 6" pieces of ribbon onto binder ring.

## time-saving tip

### Planned Spontaneity

Cut paper scraps from other projects into $2\frac{5}{8}$"x $3\frac{3}{4}$" pieces and store them with extra baseball card protectors in a zip-top plastic bag. You'll be prepared to create one of these little treasures on the spur of the moment.

# Sweet Cheeks

## Materials

- Acid-free adhesives: craft glue, dispenser
- Cardstock: coordinating colors, white
- Chipboard
- Cosmetic sponge
- Craft scissors
- Eyelet
- Eyelet setting tools
- Hole punch: $\frac{3}{16}$"
- Inkpad: white
- Ribbon: $\frac{1}{8}$" (2'); $\frac{1}{4}$" (1 yard)
- Scoring tool
- Scrapbook paper: coordinating (2); double-sided (1)
- Stickers: letters

## Instructions

1. **To create covers:** Cut two 4"x 7" pieces of chipboard and two 6"x 9" pieces of scrapbook paper. Cover chipboard pieces with paper pieces, mitering corners and adhering onto back side.

2. Cut two $3\frac{3}{4}$"x $6\frac{3}{4}$" pieces of coordinating scrapbook paper and adhere to back side of covers, covering the raw edges.

3. Cut 3"x 7" piece of coordinating cardstock. Tear thin strip from both long sides. Score and crease cardstock lengthwise at $1\frac{3}{8}$" and $1\frac{5}{8}$" to create spine for pages. Ink edges with white ink and cosmetic sponge; allow to dry.

4. Adhere chipboard covers onto inside of spine on either side of $\frac{1}{4}$" gusset. Embellish cover with letter stickers.

## time-saving tip

### Double-Duty Paper

If you don't have double-sided paper for a project or can't find the right combination of prints, simply make your own by adhering two coordinating pieces together using an adhesive application machine.

day of fun and

at Disneyland,

ked up at me with

in her eye and said,

Roxi, this is a very very

very VERY special

Yes Ashley, and you

ry very VERY special

Ashley Renee Ch

**Above:** Tell your story using computer journaling; there are a myriad of fonts to fit every theme. **Opposite:** A photograph cut into pieces that focuses on pertinent elements is a fun way to draw the eye of the viewer.

5. **To create pages:** Cut three 6¾"x 8" rectangles (two from cardstock and one from double-sided scrapbook paper). Score and fold in half, creating 6¾"x 4" pages. Nest pages inside of gusset with scrapbook paper between cardstock layers.

6. Punch two holes, 1" from top and 1" from bottom, through all pages and gusset using hole punch. Thread ⅛" ribbon length through holes and tie on inside of book.

7. **To create pocket page:** Cut 4" square of cardstock or scrapbook paper in half diagonally, forming a triangle. Punch hole and set eyelet in upturned corner, securing pocket. Embellish as desired and adhere onto page, leaving one side open to hold tags or photos.

8. Wrap ¼" ribbon vertically around book, 1" from right edge. Center and adhere ribbon on back cover using craft glue; allow to dry. Tie bow on front cover.

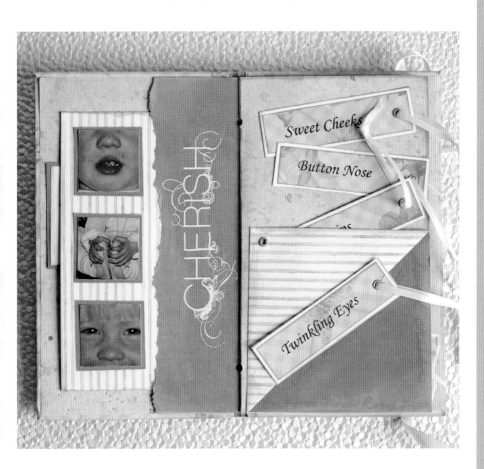

# Soccer

## Materials

- Acid-free glue stick
- Binder ring: 1¾"
- Coasters: square (6)
- Cosmetic sponge
- Craft scissors
- Decoupage medium
- Eyelet setting tools
- Eyelets: ³⁄₁₆" black (6)
- Foam brush
- Hole punch: ³⁄₁₆"
- Inkpad: green
- Ribbon: black with theme-related words (12")
- Scrapbook paper: soccer-themed
- Tissue paper: brown

## Instructions

1. **To create pages:** Cover coasters with tissue paper using decoupage medium and foam brush; allow to dry.

2. Cut six 3½" squares of soccer-themed scrapbook paper and ink edges with inkpad and cosmetic sponge; adhere to both sides of each coaster.

3. Embellish each page as desired. Apply coat of decoupage medium over each completed page; allow to dry.

4. Measuring diagonally ½" from top left corner, punch hole in first page and then attach eyelet. Using the first page as a template, repeat with remaining pages.

5. **To assemble book:** Layer pages in desired sequence and insert binder ring through eyelets. Tie two 6" lengths of ribbon onto binder ring.

## time-saving tip

### Quick Coasters

Make your own coasters by cutting 4" squares from heavy chipboard. Round the corners by snipping with scissors and then smooth the edges with sandpaper.

# School Days

## Materials

- Acid-free adhesives: double-sided tape, glue stick
- Acrylic paint: red
- Brad: square
- Cardstock: black, white
- Chipboard book: 6"x 2¾"
- Craft scissors
- Foam brush
- Inkpad: white
- Paper punch: corner rounder
- Piercing tool
- Ribbon: black scrap
- Rubber stamps: alphabet
- Scrapbook papers: various school-themed (7)

## Instructions

1. Paint all edges of chipboard book with red acrylic paint and foam brush; allow to dry.

2. Cut 12"x 2¾" strip of scrapbook paper, round corners, and adhere to book cover using double-sided tape.

3. Cut 4½"x 2½" piece of white cardstock and 4"x 2" piece of black cardstock; round corners of both pieces. Stamp title on black cardstock; mat on white cardstock. Pierce hole in upper right corner of white cardstock mat and attach ribbon scrap using brad. Center and adhere title onto front of book using glue stick; embellish as desired.

4. Cut eighteen 5½"x 2¾" pieces of coordinating scrapbook paper and round corners to match book edges. Adhere paper piece to each page using glue stick and embellish as desired.

## time-saving tip

### Thoughtful Creativity

Embellish the cover and pages of a project ahead of time as a gift. Allow the recipient to complete the book using his or her own photos, handwriting, and special memorabilia.

# Chase Brothers

## Materials

- Acid-free adhesives: craft glue, dispenser
- Burlap (6")
- Cardstock: coordinating colors (2)
- Chipboard
- Cosmetic sponges
- Craft scissors
- Embellishments: buckle, letter tiles, others as desired
- Inkpads: coordinating colors (2)
- Photos
- Scoring tool
- Scrapbook paper: double-sided coordinating colors and patterns (3)
- Stapler and staples
- Tags (4)

## Instructions

*Note:* Ink all paper element edges with coordinating ink and cosmetic sponges before assembling.

1. **To create covers:** Cut two 4½"x 5½" pieces of chipboard and two 6½"x 7½" pieces of scrapbook paper. Cover chipboard with paper, mitering corners and adhering onto back side using adhesive dispenser.

2. Thread 6" strip of burlap through buckle. Attach letter tiles and buckle to cover using craft glue; allow to dry.

3. **To create accordion:** Cut two 12"x 5" pieces of cardstock; score every 4" and fold, creating 4"x 5" accordion panels. Overlap last panel of one accordion onto first panel of second accordion; adhere together using adhesive dispenser. Adhere first panel of accordion to back side of cover. Repeat with remaining panel and cover. Embellish as desired.

4. **To create pockets:** Fold bottom third of each tag and staple in place, creating pockets. Embellish pages as desired.

# Grandma's Masterpieces

## Materials

- Acid-free adhesive dispenser
- Artwork: children's drawings (5)
- Brads (5)
- Cardstock: coordinating colors
- Chipboard
- Craft scissors
- Hole punch: $\frac{1}{4}$"
- Library pockets: $3\frac{1}{2}$"x 5", coordinating colors (5)
- Piercing tool
- Ribbon: $\frac{1}{4}$" grosgrain coordinating colors (4)
- Scoring tool
- Scrapbook paper: coordinating colors and patterns (2)

## Instructions

1. **To create covers:** Cut two $3\frac{1}{2}$"x $5\frac{3}{4}$" pieces of chipboard and two $4\frac{1}{2}$"x $6\frac{3}{4}$" pieces of coordinating scrapbook paper. Cover chipboard with paper, mitering corners and adhering onto back side.

2. **To create accordion binding:** Cut one $3\frac{1}{2}$"x 8" piece of cardstock; score every $\frac{1}{2}$" and fold, beginning with valley fold. Adhere accordion ends to back side of covers using adhesive dispenser. *Note:* Align accordion with right edge of front cover and left edge of back cover. Cut two $3\frac{1}{4}$"x $5\frac{1}{2}$" pieces of cardstock; adhere to inside of covers.

3. **To create pages:** Scan and reduce artwork to $2\frac{3}{4}$"x $4\frac{1}{4}$". Cut five $5\frac{1}{2}$" x $3\frac{1}{4}$" pieces of cardstock; trim corners on one narrow end, creating tag shape. Center and punch $\frac{1}{4}$" holes in tag top; adhere artwork to cardstock. Cut five 5" lengths of coordinating ribbons; fold in half. Pierce ribbon with piercing tool. Thread brad through holes in folded ribbon and tag; open prongs and flatten to secure.

4. **To assemble book:** Print journaling on coordinating cardstock and trim to $5\frac{1}{2}$"x $3\frac{1}{2}$"; adhere to first valley fold of spine. Adhere sealed ends of library pockets to remaining valley folds using adhesive dispenser. Tuck artwork tags into pockets. Embellish cover with title matted on coordinating cardstock. Wrap 1 yard of ribbon around book and tie bow on front.

# Four Steps to Success

## Materials

- Acid-free adhesives: double-sided tape, foam mounting tape, glue stick
- Cardstock: brown
- Cosmetic sponge
- Craft knife
- Craft scissors
- Elastic hair band: black
- Hole punches: ¼", 1¼" square
- Inkpad: brown
- Photo
- Rub-ons: words
- Scoring tool
- Scrapbook paper: coordinating (3)
- Stick: 6"

## Instructions

1. **To create cover:** Cut 6"x 12" piece of coordinating scrapbook paper and two 6"x 12" pieces of cardstock. Score and fold paper and cardstock pieces in half; place cardstock pages inside paper cover.

2. Punch three squares on right side of paper, ¾" from edge. Outline squares with foam mounting tape on inside of cover. Place photo behind squares; adhere front cover panel to first cardstock page using double-sided tape. Tear edges of remaining three brown pages.

3. **To create pages:** Cut eight 6" squares of coordinating scrapbook papers; adhere one square each onto inside front and back covers. Tear one edge of each remaining square approximately ⅛" narrower than cardstock pages. Ink edges of torn squares with inkpad and cosmetic sponge; adhere to cardstock using double-sided tape. Embellish as desired.

4. **To create binding:** Punch two ¼" holes in covers and pages, ½" in from left edge at 1" and 5" from top. Thread elastic hair band through holes from back and loop over stick ends. Embellish cover as desired.

# Tooth Fairy Box

## Materials

- Acid-free adhesive dispenser
- Acrylic paint: off-white
- Brad: brass
- Cardstock: coordinating colors
- Chipboard
- Cosmetic sponges
- Craft scissors
- Foam brush
- Hole punch: $\frac{1}{8}$"
- Inkpads: coordinating colors
- Matchbox: small
- Ribbon: $\frac{1}{8}$" white organdy (18")
- Scoring tool
- Scrapbook paper

## Instructions

*Note:* Ink edges of all paper elements using inkpads and cosmetic sponge before assembling. Let ink dry thoroughly between each application.

1. Paint matchbox drawer with acrylic paint and foam brush; allow to dry.

2. Cut two $2\frac{1}{2}$"x $1\frac{3}{4}$" pieces of chipboard and two $3\frac{1}{2}$"x $2\frac{3}{4}$" pieces of scrapbook paper. Cover chipboard shapes with paper, mitering corners towards back side of board. Adhere using adhesive dispenser.

3. Cut $2\frac{1}{16}$"x 4" piece of cardstock. Wrap and adhere cardstock strip around matchbox sleeve.

4. Sandwich matchbox sleeve between mitered sides of covered book boards and adhere.

5. **To create accordion:** Cut 2"x 12" piece of cardstock. Score and fold at $1\frac{1}{2}$" increments, creating an accordion. Center and adhere accordion to top of box assemblage. Cut $1\frac{1}{4}$"x $1\frac{3}{4}$" piece of scrapbook paper and adhere to top of accordion.

6. Punch hole in center of drawer front using hole punch. Insert brad and flatten prongs onto back of drawer front.

7. Embellish pages as desired. Wrap box and book with ribbon and adhere to underside of box. Tie bow on top of book.

## CHAPTER 4

What better way could there be to capture the essence of love than with a handmade miniature book? You can tell the story of undying devotion between your grandparents, celebrate your first year together, or write a love letter to your soulmate within the pages of one of these little treasures. In this chapter you'll find inspiration to document many types of affections, from puppy love to your passion for a hobby, to the dedication between two parents. When we take the time to look about and count the blessings in our lives, we find the perfect subjects to build our own love stories on. Creating one of these projects that tells a story will bring joy to your heart and fill the hearts of those you love.

# You Are . . .

## Materials

- Acid-free double-sided tape
- Brads (2)
- Cardstock: black, tan
- Chipboard
- Cosmetic sponge
- Craft scissors
- Eyelet setting tools
- Eyelets: bronze (8)
- Fiber: hemp twine
- Hole punch: $\frac{1}{2}$"
- Inkpad: black
- Piercing tool
- Scoring tool
- Scrapbook papers: coordinating prints (3)

## Instructions

1. **To create covers:** Cut two 4"x6" pieces of chipboard; trim corners from one short end of each rectangle, creating tag shapes. Cut two 5"x7" pieces of scrapbook paper and adhere to tags. Miter and adhere paper corners onto back side of tag. Embellish covers with coordinating scrapbook papers.

2. **To create pages:** Using cover as a template, trace two tag shapes onto coordinating scrapbook paper and four tags slightly smaller than covers onto tan cardstock. Cut inside traced lines and ink edges with black inkpad and cosmetic sponge. Adhere paper tags onto back of each cover.

3. **To assemble book:** Cut one 8$\frac{1}{2}$"x4" piece of black cardstock. Score at 1$\frac{1}{4}$" then in $\frac{3}{4}$" increments for eight additional spots, leaving 1$\frac{1}{4}$" at end of strip. Fold cardstock on scored lines, creating accordion binding. Adhere left side of accordion folds together.

4. Mark and set eight eyelets at $\frac{1}{2}$" increments along each short end of accordion binding. Insert one cover into first valley fold and the other into last valley fold on binding and adhere. Insert and adhere tags to each valley fold in binding.

5. Punch two $\frac{1}{2}$" circles from black cardstock. Pierce starter holes and attach a circle to right center edge of each cover using brads. Wrap 8" piece of hemp twine around circle on back cover and knot. Wrap other end of twine around front circle to close album. Embellish cover and pages as desired.

# Key to My Heart

## Materials

- Acid-free adhesives: dispenser, double-sided tape, vellum tape
- Cardstock: antique gold metallic, cream
- Craft knife
- Craft scissors
- Embellishments: 2½" metal slide mount, skeleton key
- Embossing powder: gold
- Foam core board
- Heat tool
- Hole punch: ¼"
- Metal-edge ruler
- Paper punch: 1" square
- Pens: copper leafing, embossing
- Ribbon: 1½" antique gold satin (24")
- Scrapbook paper: coordinating patterns
- Vellum: gold

## Instructions

1. **To create covers:** Cut two 4"x 7" pieces of foam core board using craft knife and metal-edge ruler. Cut and adhere two 6"x 9" pieces of gold metallic cardstock and cover foam core boards, mitering corners onto back of board. Punch holes in each board, ¾" from side and ½" from top.

2. Cut 2" square of gold vellum. Draw heart on vellum with embossing pen. Sprinkle heart with gold embossing powder and heat with heat tool until powder is melted.

3. Paint metal slide mount using copper leafing pen; allow to dry. Mount vellum square under slide mount then onto front cover using double-sided tape.

4. **To create pages:** Cut eight 3¾"x 6½" pieces of cream cardstock. Print photos and journaling onto vellum and trim to fit pages. Mat journaling boxes using cream cardstock and vellum tape.

5. Punch ten 1" squares of textured gold paper. Cut each square diagonally, creating four triangles; adhere onto corners of photos and journaling boxes with adhesive dispenser.

6. **To assemble book:** Assemble pages in desired order. Punch ¼" holes in pages, using cover as a guide. Thread ribbon through all layers and tie in front.

*our
first
year

OXOXOXOX

# Our First Year

## Materials

- Acid-free double-sided tape
- Brad: antique brass
- Cardstock: off-white
- CD of photos with blank label
- Craft scissors
- Hole punch: ⅛"
- Paper punch: corner rounder
- Pencil
- Ribbon: ¼" satin (32")
- Scoring tool
- Scrapbook paper: coordinating colors and patterns

## Instructions

1. **To create cover:** Cut one 5"x 12" and two 5½"x 4⅞" pieces of cardstock. Score lines on large piece across short width 3⅞" from top, 4" from top, and 3" from bottom. On each smaller piece, score line across short width 1" from one edge. (See Diagram.)

2. Adhere flaps of shorter pieces to either side of middle section of large piece. *Note:* Project will resemble cross, with shortest flap at bottom. (See Diagram.) Score and fold all creases. Round all outside corners with paper punch.

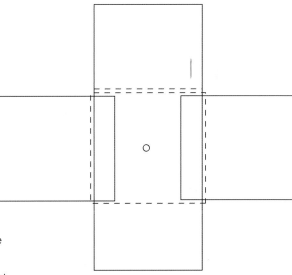

3. Open project completely and mark center of middle section using CD as a template; punch hole. Insert brad through back of book and open prongs to hold CD.

love [luv] v. 1. a pass
affection; for a sweet
2. deep devotion 3. w
will always feel for you,
is a verb make me imm
with a kiss. - You are e
thing I never knew I always wanted—
give all to love, obey thy heart— is
romantic? you & me together forev
happily ever after... how do I love the
me count the ways – *Shakespeare* the hea
do anything – *nature* love is, in its
essence, spiritual fire. – *Seneca* you're
the love of my life – our romance
I LOVE YOU I LOVE YOU I LO

xoxoxoxoxoxoxoxoxoxoxoxoxoxoxoxoxoxoxoxox
xoxoxoxoxoxoxoxoxoxoxoxoxoxoxoxoxox

TOGETHER IS THE NICEST

marci
lambert

happy anniversary!
here's a year's worth
of my favorite photos
so we'll never forget
what a great time
we had.
♡ love ♡

**Above:** Flaps provide perfect spots to add photos as a preview for what you'll find on the CD. **Opposite:** Embellish the CD label with computer-generated or handwritten journaling and rub-on flourishes.

4. Center and adhere ribbon just below hole on middle section. Embellish inside panels, CD, and cover as desired.

5. Fold side flaps in, bottom flap up, and top flap down. Tie ribbon to close book.

## time-saving tip

### Edge Options

Use a coordinating ink color to cover the cut edges of paper and photos. Using an ink pad directly on the paper's edges results in a sharp-looking edge, while inking with a cosmetic sponge creates a softer effect. You can even color the edges with a felt-tip pen.

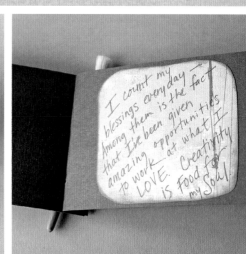

# Love What You Do

## Materials

- Acid-free glue stick
- Cardstock: blue (2)
- Elastic hair band: black
- Hole punch: ¼"
- Marker: fine-point, black
- Monogram letters: 3½" lowercase, coordinating colors and patterns
- Paintbrush: 5"
- Scoring tool
- Vellum: white

## Instructions

1. **To create pages:** Cut three 4"x 9" pieces of cardstock. Score one piece at 1" and 2"; fold at 2" score. Score second piece at 2" and 3"; fold at 3". Score third piece at 3" and 4"; fold at 4". Nest folded pieces together, creating stair-step pages. Fold top piece at 1" score line and tuck back under itself to reinforce binding.

2. **To create cover:** Cut 4"x 7" piece of vellum; center and score 3¾"x 6¾" rectangle. Tuck vellum under top fold of cardstock with raised rectangle facing up. Embellish cover as desired.

3. Punch hole ¼" in from folded edge and 1" from top; punch second hole ¾" in from folded edge and 3" from top. Thread elastic hair band through holes from back and loop over paintbrush. Write desired words on vellum edges.

4. Adhere monogram letters onto right edges of staggered pages. Embellish pages as desired.

## time-saving tip

### Create Your Own Monograms

Make your own monogram letters in the font size and style you need. Type the desired letters in a large font size (a 520 point size yields approximately 3½"-high letters) and print onto plain paper. Adhere template to cardstock, chipboard, or scrapbook paper with removable adhesive and cut out.

# To Have and To Hold

## Materials

- Acid-free adhesives: craft glue, double-sided tape

- Chipboard

- Craft scissors

- Ribbon: 1½" off-white satin (2½ yards)

- Scrapbook paper: floral print

## Instructions

1. **To create covers and pages:** Cut seven 4"x5" pieces of chipboard and seven 5"x6" pieces of scrapbook paper. Cover chipboard with paper, mitering corners to back side; adhere with double-sided tape.

2. **To assemble book:** Position covered chipboard pieces face down in a vertical row with ½" gaps between pieces. Cut 2-yard length of ribbon. Center ribbon down row of panels with 3" extending past top panel and 22" beyond bottom panel. Adhere using craft glue; allow to dry. Loop 3" top section back on itself, creating ¼" decorative loop, and adhere with craft glue; allow to dry.

3. Adhere 18" piece of ribbon over bottom panel ribbon. *Note:* This length will be tied around book to hold it closed. Embellish cover and panels as desired.

## time-saving tip

### Embellished Options

Instead of tracking down the exact color of brads and other metal embellishments called for in the project directions, use leafing pens to transform items you have on hand to coordinate with your projects.

# My Blessings

## Materials

- Acid-free glue stick
- Cardstock: coordinating colors
- Cosmetic sponge
- Craft scissors
- Envelopes: 5¾" x 4⅜" (5)
- Hole punch: ¼"
- Inkpad: brown
- Photos (4)
- Ribbon: ⅞" brown check (1 yard)
- Scrapbook paper: coordinating colors and patterns

## Instructions

*Note:* All paper elements are inked with brown ink and a cosmetic sponge before assembling.

1. **To create accordion:** Moisten envelope flap and adhere onto front of second envelope. *Note:* The envelope flap crease should sit slightly below the bottom of the previous envelope. Repeat with remaining envelopes.

2. Cut piece of scrapbook paper using envelope flap as template; adhere liner to inside of top envelope flap. Punch ¼" hole ½" from top edge in center of lined flap; thread ribbon through hole.

3. Cut five 5½" x 4¼" pieces of cardstock. Add journaling and embellishments to cards as desired; tuck inside envelopes. Mat photos with coordinating cardstock and adhere onto envelopes.

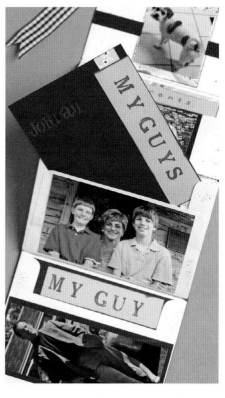

4. Fold envelopes so top flap will overlap bottom envelope opening. Embellish front and back of folded accordion as desired. Wrap ribbon around book and tie to close.

# All You Need is Love

## Materials

- Acid-free adhesives: dispenser, double-sided tape
- Acrylic paint: coordinating color
- Charm: heart
- Chipboard
- Computer and printer
- Craft scissors
- Foam brush
- Quotes: love-themed
- Ribbon: 1" gold organdy (18")
- Scrapbook paper: double-sided, single-sided, coordinating colors and patterns (2 each)
- Transparency sheet

## Instructions

1. **To create covers:** Cut two 4½"x 3⅜" pieces of chipboard and two 6½"x 5⅜" pieces of coordinating single-sided scrapbook paper. Cover chipboard with paper, mitering corners and adhering onto back side using adhesive dispenser.

2. **To create accordion:** Cut two 4"x 12" pieces of double-sided scrapbook paper. Score and fold in 3" increments. Measure and mark middle of one end panel. Cut folded accordion through all layers from center of one 3" edge to ⅛" past marked center point. Repeat with remaining accordion. Open accordions and weave cut sides together, creating a honeycomb.

3. **To embellish pages:** Type five theme-related quotes no larger than 1⅜"x 3" and one quote no larger than 2"x 2½". Print onto transparency sheet and trim to desired size. Paint light strokes of acrylic paint onto backside of quotes, using foam brush; allow to dry. Adhere smaller quotes to honeycomb as desired using adhesive dispenser.

4. Mat large quote with coordinating scrapbook paper; adhere onto front cover. Center and adhere ribbon across width of mitered side of back cover using double-sided tape; trim ends. Center and adhere ends of honeycomb accordion onto inside covers using double-sided tape. Thread heart charm onto ribbon; tie bow on front cover.

# Celebrating 50 Years

## Materials

- Acid-free adhesives: dispenser, double-sided tape, glue stick
- Cardstock: ivory
- Chipboard
- Craft scissors
- Craft wire: gold
- Eyelet setting tools
- Eyelets: gold (12)
- Leafing pen: gold
- Needle-nose pliers
- Ribbon: ¼" coordinating color; ¼" satin (2')
- Scrapbook paper: wedding-themed
- Seed beads: white

## Instructions

1. **To create covers:** Cut two 4" octagons from chipboard and two 4½" pieces of scrapbook paper. Cover chipboard with paper, mitering and adhering corners onto back side of covers with adhesive dispenser.

2. Cut two 12" lengths of satin ribbon. Center and adhere first 2" of one piece of ribbon to unfinished side of cover using double-sided tape. Repeat with second cover.

3. Cut six 4" octagons from ivory cardstock. Edge all pages on both sides with gold leafing pen. Adhere cardstock octagon onto each cover's unfinished side, securing ribbon.

4. On each cover, at straight edge directly opposite of ribbon lengths, set two eyelets ¼" in from edge and ¼" down from each corner. Set eyelet in pages using same measurements. Layer covers with pages inside.

5. Thread wire through eyelets and twist together loosely. String seed beads onto wire and curl ends with pliers.

6. Embellish pages and cover as desired.

## time-saving tip

### Quick Embellishments
Save favors from a 50th anniversary party or a wedding reception and use as embellishments to personalize a special miniature book.

A friend
is one of the
nicest things
you can have,
and one of the
best things
you can be.
—Douglas Pagels

# CHAPTER 5

True friends are always there when you need them, laughing and crying with you through life's ups and downs. They laugh at your jokes, and make you feel as comfortable as your favorite pair of slippers. Friendships can develop during childhood and last a lifetime while others seem to come around at just the perfect moments in our lives. Some valued friendships are of the four-legged type, some are the kind we can tell our deepest secrets to, while others we depend on to lift our spirits. Show your kindred spirits how much they mean to you by sharing memories and sentiments in the form of a small book. The ideas presented in this chapter will help you create projects as unique and special as your own treasured friendships.

I'LL GET BY WITH **LOTS** OF HELP FROM **MY FRIENDS!**

# I'll Get By

## Materials

- Acid-free adhesive dispenser
- Cardstock: black, off-white, orange
- Chalk inkpad: black
- Chipboard
- Computer and printer
- Cosmetic sponge
- Craft scissors
- Paper punch: ½" circle
- Ribbon: ⅜" orange (24")
- Scoring tool
- Scrapbook paper: black-and-cream

## Instructions

1. **To create covers:** Cut two 3¼" squares of chipboard and two 4¼" squares of black-and-cream scrapbook paper. Cover chipboard with paper, mitering corners and adhering onto back side of chipboard. Ink edges with black chalk ink and cosmetic sponge.

2. **To create accordion:** Cut three 3"x 12" strips of black cardstock; score and fold in 3" increments to create accordions. Adhere last section of one folded strip onto first section of next strip; add sections as desired. Adhere first and last pages of completed accordion onto back sides of covers.

3. Center ribbon so ends extend 10" beyond either side of front cover; adhere to front cover.

4. Cut 3" square of orange cardstock and 2⅞" square of black cardstock. Type first and last line of title in 2¾" square text box, leaving space between lines to fit "LOTS." Print and trim to size; ink edges.

5. Print word "LOTS" in larger font than rest of title. Make sure to leave space around each letter so that it can be punched out with circle punch; ink edges. Adhere onto title block as desired.

6. Layer and adhere orange square, black square, and printed square. Adhere to front cover covering ribbon. Embellish pages as desired.

# Best Buds

## Materials

- Acid-free adhesives: double-sided tape, glue stick
- Brads: mini (2)
- Buttons (2)
- Craft scissors
- Hole punch: ¼"
- Piercing tool
- Ribbon: ½" coordinating colors and patterns (2–3)
- Scoring tool
- Scrapbook paper: double-sided coordinating colors and patterns (4)
- String: black (3")
- Transparency sheet: 4⅜"x 5¾" printed

## Instructions

1. Cut two envelopes from double-sided scrapbook paper using Envelope Template on page 91; score folds.

2. Cut left flap from one envelope. Adhere top flap onto bottom using glue stick; embellish as desired.

3. Fold top and bottom flaps closed on second envelope but do not adhere; embellish as desired. Open flaps; embellish inside panel. Fold left flap in and lay transparency sheet on top; adhere with double-sided tape. Adhere right flap of first envelope on top of transparency.

## time-saving tip

### Envelope Ideas

Carefully disassemble a ready-made envelope to use as a template for creating different shaped mini-books in the same format as this project. Many scrapbook stores have die-cutting systems and envelope dies available for use that allow you to make a large number of envelopes quickly and easily.

**Top:** Boyhood friendship is documented in this mini-book created with two envelopes cut from templates. **Above:** Open the flaps to reveal the innocence of young buddies, embellished with a printed transparency overlay.

4. Fold in bottom and top flaps of right envelope. Fold left envelope over onto right; fold remaining flap onto front. Pierce starter hole in middle of right-side flap. Center brad and insert prongs into hole through button; flatten prongs onto back side of flap. Repeat with remaining brad and button 1" left of first button. Tie string around base of one button and wrap around second button to close.

5. Cut one 4"x 5½" piece of scrapbook paper. Trim two corners from one end, creating tag. Punch hole in tag top; thread 6" length of ribbon through hole and knot. Embellish tag as desired; insert into pocket on left envelope.

6. Embellish cover as desired.

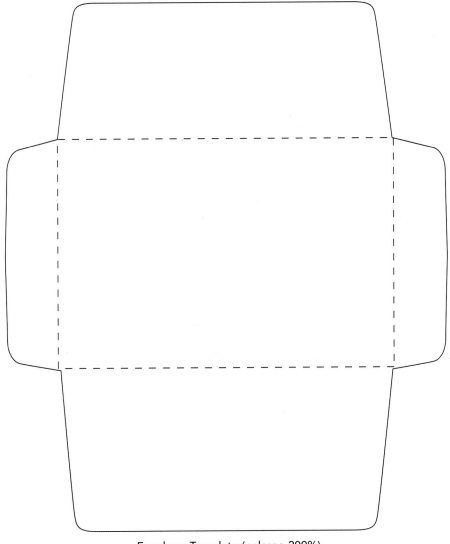

Envelope Template (enlarge 200%)

# Dogs Complete Life

## Materials

- Acid-free adhesives: dispenser, double-sided tape
- Acrylic paint: red
- Artist canvas panels: 5"x7" (4)
- Cardstock: black, red, white
- Cosmetic sponge
- Craft scissors
- Dog collar: small
- Foam brush
- Hole punch: $\frac{1}{4}$"
- Inkpad: black
- Paper punches: corner rounder, photo corner
- Ribbon: assortment of red, white-and-black
- Scrapbook paper: black, red, coordinating patterns

## Instructions

1. **To create accordion:** Paint sides and edges of canvas panels using acrylic paint and foam brush; allow to dry. Lightly ink edges with inkpad and cosmetic sponge.

2. Cut seven 3"x4⅜" pieces of black cardstock. Apply double-sided tape to three sides of cardstock piece, leaving one long edge open, creating pocket. Adhere pocket ½" from bottom of canvas. Repeat with remaining six cardstock pieces and both sides of panels. *Note:* One panel will be the front cover of the book.

3. **To create pockets:** Cut seven 2¾"x4" pieces of scrapbook paper. Ink edges with black inkpad and cosmetic sponge; adhere paper onto each pocket with double-sided tape. Embellish pockets with ribbon.

4. Line up panels in preferred order. Cut six 2"x3" strips of coordinating scrapbook paper; adhere wrong sides together using adhesive dispenser. Fold hinges in half, matching short sides.

## Quick Quips

**Save time creating journaling boxes and titles by printing text directly onto the cardstock, then trim to desired size.**

**Top:** Each panel is created following the same format and then each pocket and tag is embellished. **Above:** Unusual elements such as this dog collar and tags make a clever book closure.

**Left:** Coordinating paper strips create hinges between the panels, allowing the mini-book to be accordion folded.

5. **To assemble book:** Using double-sided tape, adhere hinges onto first two panels, 1" from top and bottom, maintaining ⅜" gaps between panels. Repeat with third and fourth panels. Turn panels over; adhere hinges between second and third panels using same placement as previous hinges.

6. Cut seven 3½"x 6" pieces of black cardstock. Round top corners using paper punch. Punch ¼" holes in top center of tags. Cut seven 6" lengths of coordinating ribbon; thread length through hole and knot.

7. Punch photos with photo corner punch; mat on red cardstock and mount on tags. Embellish as desired. Use dog collar as closure.

## Short-Order Design
Replace all pockets with purchased library pockets and tags, which are available at many office supply stores.

# Stamp Club Friends

## Materials

- Acid-free craft glue
- Cardstock: light tan
- Chipboard
- Craft scissors
- Foam brush
- Handmade paper: coordinating colors
- Hole punch: $\frac{1}{8}$"
- Inkpads: black, green, orange, rust
- Rubber stamps: flowers, friendship quotes, harlequin, hearts, leaves
- Waxed thread

## Instructions

1. **To create covers:** Cut two 6"x 9" pieces of handmade paper. Cut two 6"x 4" and two 1"x 4" pieces of chipboard. Lay one paper piece face down on work surface. Apply craft glue to paper using foam brush. Place one 6"x 4" and one 1"x 4" chipboard piece on paper, centering between paper's top and bottom, leaving $\frac{3}{16}$" gap between pieces. Miter paper corners onto back side. Repeat with second set of chipboard pieces and paper.

2. Cut two 3½"x 7" pieces of coordinating paper and adhere onto back side of covers; embellish as desired.

3. **To create pages:** Cut six 6¾"x 3¾" pieces of light tan cardstock. Stamp backgrounds on cardstock pages using rubber stamps and inkpads; embellish as desired.

4. Measure, mark, and punch binding holes on front cover ½" from left side, 1" and 3" from top. Punch holes on back cover and pages using front cover as template.

5. **To assemble book:** Stack covers and pages together; bind using waxed thread and stab-binding technique.

## time-saving tip

### Drilling Holes
Quickly create binding holes through multiple layers by clipping pages and covers together with binder clips. Use a rotary tool to drill the holes.

MAN'S
BEST
FRIENDS

This is one of Grandpa Murphy's top producing Jersey cows named Juno. Also in the picture is her 3 day old calf Irma. This was on a dairy farm in Martinsville, Indiana.

1929

# Man's Best Friends

## Materials

- Acid-free adhesive dispenser
- Acrylic paint: light blue
- Copper post fasteners
- Cosmetic sponge
- Craft scissors
- Foam brush
- Hole punch: ¼"
- Inkpads: brown, light blue
- Rubber stamp: chicken wire background
- Scoring tool
- Scrapbook paper: striped
- Tags: 6¼"x 3⅛" white (11)
- Yarn: coordinating color

## Instructions

1. **To create pages:** Lightly brush watered-down acrylic paint onto tags with foam brush; allow to dry. Stamp tags with chicken wire background stamp and light blue ink.

2. Cut eleven 3⅛"x 6" pieces of scrapbook paper. Fold each piece in half, matching short ends; center fold over flat end of tag and adhere with adhesive dispenser. Ink tag with brown inkpad and cosmetic sponge.

3. Score 1" from square end of tag; crease. Embellish tags as desired.

4. **To assemble book:** Punch holes in left edge of tags ½" from outside edge and ½" from top and bottom; insert copper post fasteners. Cut eleven 6" lengths of yarn and thread one through hole in each tag; knot.

## time-saving tip

### Hole How-Tos

**Save time by measuring and marking hole placement on the cover tag. You can then use the tag as a template for the remaining tags.**

# Girlfriends

## Materials

- Acid-free adhesives: bookbinding tape, double-sided tape, glue stick
- Chipboard
- Cosmetic sponges
- Craft scissors
- Inkpads: coordinating colors
- Ribbon: ⅝" coordinating color (1 yard)
- Scrapbook paper: coordinating colors and patterns (6)
- Stickers: quotes

## Instructions

1. **To create accordion:** Cut six 4"x6" pieces of chipboard and ten 6" strips of bookbinding tape. Lay panels side-by-side, long sides together, leaving ⅛" gap between each; adhere together using tape strips. Turn connected panels face down and adhere strips between panels on back side. Ink edges of all panels and tape strips using coordinating inkpads and cosmetic sponges.

2. **To create binding:** Cut two 18" lengths of ribbon. Center 3" of ribbon end vertically and adhere to outside of front panel using double-sided tape. Repeat with remaining ribbon and back panel.

3. Cut twelve 4"x6" pieces of scrapbook paper; ink edges and adhere to each side of all panels using glue stick. Embellish panels as desired.

## time-saving tip

### Smoothing out the Rough Spots

Use a sanding block or nail file to smooth edges of chipboard pieces. This is also a quick and easy method of distressing scrapbook paper.

# Childhood Friends

## Materials

- Acid-free adhesives: dispenser, glue stick
- Cardstock: off-white
- Craft scissors
- Dental floss threader
- Hole punch: $\frac{1}{16}$"
- Paper bags: $3\frac{1}{2}$" x $6\frac{1}{2}$" brown (3)
- Pencil
- Scrapbook paper: coordinating colors and prints
- Thread: heavyweight light green

## Instructions

1. **To create covers:** Cut one 4"x 8" piece each of scrapbook paper and cardstock. Adhere wrong sides together using glue stick and fold in half to make 4"-square cover.

2. **To create paper bag pages:** Layer three paper bags together, alternating ends; fold in half crosswise and unfold. Center and align cover on top of unfolded bags. Mark 1" in from top and bottom on cover fold; punch two $\frac{1}{16}$" holes through all layers. *Note:* It may be easier to punch one layer at a time using the cover as a template.

3. **To bind book:** Pull thread through holes using dental floss threader as needle. Tie bow on outside book spine. Embellish cover and pages as desired.

# Best Friends Forever

## Materials

- Acid-free craft glue
- Ball chain with closure: 3" (2)
- Chipboard
- Cosmetic sponge
- Craft scissors
- Eyelet setting tools
- Eyelets: ¼" flower (24)
- Foam brush
- Inkpad: black
- Sandpaper
- Scrapbook paper: coordinating colors and patterns (5–6)

## Instructions

1. Cut five 6" chipboard squares; round off one side of each square with scissors. Cut ten pieces of scrapbook paper using chipboard piece as template.

2. Apply craft glue to chipboard surfaces using foam brush. Adhere scrapbook paper; allow to dry.

3. Sand edges of covered chipboard; ink edges using black ink and cosmetic sponge.

4. Set eyelets ½" from edge opposite curve and 1½" from top and bottom on all pages. Bind pages together using chains. Embellish cover and pages as desired.

It is one of the blessings of old friends that you can afford to be stupid with them.
Ralph Waldo Emerson

## CHAPTER 6

Birthdays come around every year, whether we like it or not. Among the projects in this chapter you will find an array of small birthday-themed books filled with fun twists and interesting formats. Celebrate the anticipation of a birth or chronicle parties for all types of people, young and old alike. Mini-books are a unique way to capture birthday memories, and they can become thoughtful and unique gifts. Some can even be turned into interesting décor pieces to be proudly displayed in your home, while others can provide an unusual way to deliver gift cards and gift certificates. Although with each passing birthday we grow a little older, we all love blowing out candles and opening gifts, especially if the gift is a book made in our honor.

planning A birthday

# Planning a Birthday

## Materials

- Acid-free double-sided tape
- Cardstock: coordinating colors (3–4)
- Cosmetic sponges
- Craft scissors
- Eyelet setting tools
- Eyelets (2)
- Inkpads: coordinating colors
- Ribbon: ¼" gingham
- Scoring tool
- Scrapbook paper: double-sided coordinating colors and patterns (2)

## Instructions

*Note:* Ink all paper elements with coordinating inkpads and cosmetic sponges before assembling.

1. **To create matchbook cover:** Cut one 5"x 12" piece of double-sided scrapbook paper; score and fold at 1¼" and 7" from narrow end.

2. **To create accordion:** Cut two 4¾"x 11" pieces of cardstock; score and fold strips at 1" and 6" from narrow end. Adhere 1" section of one cardstock strip to back of 5" section of remaining strip, creating one long accordion.

3. Fold 1" section at end of accordion back onto itself and tuck inside 1" section of cover. Set two eyelets through flap of cover and end of accordion to secure. Thread ¼" gingham ribbon through eyelets and tie in a bow.

4. Embellish cover and pages as desired.

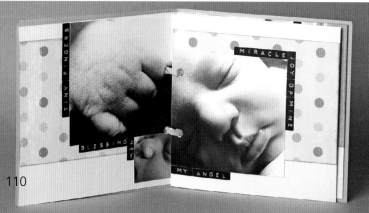

# We Welcome Henry

## Materials

- Acid-free adhesive dispenser
- Cardstock: light green, off-white
- Cosmetic sponges
- Craft scissors
- Inkpads: coordinating colors
- Paper punches: ¼" circle; 1½" square
- Pencil
- Photos: black-and-white
- Ribbon: coordinating colors (2)
- Scoring tool
- Scrapbook paper: coordinating colors and patterns (3)

## Instructions

1. **To create cover:** Cut one 6"x 12" piece of light green cardstock. Score and fold in half to form 6" square.

2. Cut two 5⅞"x 11¾" pieces of off-white cardstock. Score and fold in half to form 5⅞" square. Place cardstock pages inside light green cover with folded sides together.

3. Make pencil marks ¼" in from folded edge, and 2" and 4" from top. Punch ¼" holes at marks. *Note:* You may need to punch one layer at a time using cover as a template.

4. **To create pages:** Cut patterned paper into strips. Ink edges using coordinating colored inkpads and cosmetic sponges. Arrange and adhere paper strips and square photos onto pages. *Note:* If holes are covered with patterned paper, punch through again.

5. Embellish cover and pages as desired.

6. Cut 10" pieces of ribbon. Thread ribbon lengths through holes and knot.

## time-saving tip

### Page Pointers
Create a book with four pages instead of eight by using only one piece of off-white cardstock or increase the page count by four for each additional piece of cardstock.

# Happy Birthday

## Materials

- Acid-free adhesive dispenser
- Craft scissors
- Photos
- Scrapbook paper: double-sided coordinating colors and patterns (4)
- Spiral binding system
- Sticker letters

## Instructions

1. **To create pages and cover:** Cut seven 6" squares of double-sided scrapbook paper. Embellish one square with strips of coordinating scrapbook paper and sticker letters for cover.

2. Embellish pages as desired. Reserve last page for photo of birthday child with message.

3. Bind book using spiral binding system according to manufacturer's instructions. *Note:* If you don't have access to a spiral binding system, take the book to a copy shop to have the pages bound.

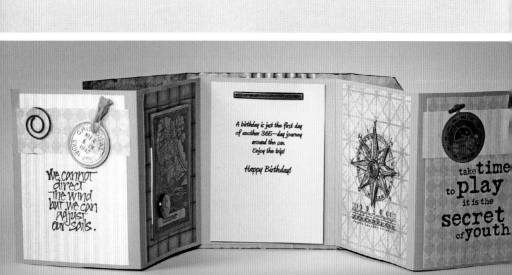

# Discover Life's Journey

## Materials

- Acid-free adhesive dispenser
- Cardstock: double-sided coordinating color
- Craft knife
- Craft scissors
- Hole punch: $\frac{1}{16}$"
- Scoring tool
- Scrapbook paper: double-sided coordinating color

## Instructions

1. **To create cover:** Cut 5"x 12" piece of double-sided cardstock; score and fold as shown. (See Diagram.) Trim right edge as shown to make cover flap. (See Diagram.)

2. Measure $2\frac{3}{8}$" from left short edge and cut slit with craft knife, ending $\frac{7}{8}$" from top and bottom of cover as shown. (See Diagram.) Punch holes at each end of slit to prevent tearing.

3. **To create accordion:** Cut two $4\frac{3}{4}$"x $11\frac{5}{8}$" strips of cardstock; score in $3\frac{7}{8}$" increments across $11\frac{5}{8}$" width and fold accordion-style. Overlap one end panel of each strip, forming one five-panel accordion; adhere together.

4. **To assemble book:** Adhere overlapped section to inside center section of cover. Embellish cover and pages as desired.

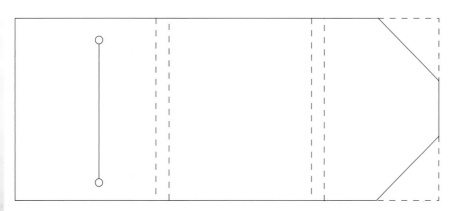

# Bowling Birthday Boy

## Materials

- Acid-free double-sided tape
- Acrylic paint: coordinating colors
- Cardstock: coordinating colors (2–3)
- Cosmetic sponge
- Craft scissors
- Foam brush
- Inkpad: coordinating colors
- Scoring tool
- Scrapbook paper: coordinating colors and patterns
- Stretched artist canvases: 5"x 7" (2)
- Twill tape: ⅜" off-white (4½')

## Instructions

1. **To create covers:** Paint canvas front and sides with acrylic paint and foam brush; allow to dry. Ink using coordinating inkpad and cosmetic sponge.

2. Cut two 5"x 7" pieces of scrapbook paper; adhere to canvas back sides using double-sided tape. Adhere twill tape to canvas edges.

3. **To create accordion:** Cut three 6½"x 9" pieces of cardstock; score and fold in half. Overlap panel of each folded cardstock piece, creating four-panel accordion; adhere together.

4. **To assemble book:** Lay canvases right side up; adhere first accordion panel onto canvas surface using double-sided tape. Repeat with remaining canvas and end panel. Embellish cover and accordion as desired.

# Happy 18th Birthday

## Materials

- Acid-free adhesives: craft glue, dispenser
- Chipboard
- Cosmetic sponge
- Craft scissors
- Foam brush
- Hole punch: $\frac{1}{4}$"
- Inkpad: brown
- Jute twine: 10"
- Sandpaper
- Scrapbook paper: coordinating colors and patterns (3–4)
- Self-adhesive hole reinforcements

## Instructions

1. **To create pages:** Cut four 5" chipboard squares and eight 5" scrapbook paper squares. Adhere paper to both sides of chipboard pages using craft glue; allow to dry.

2. Round corners with scissors and sand edges smooth; ink edges using inkpad and cosmetic sponge. Embellish pages as desired.

3. **To assemble book:** Punch hole $\frac{1}{2}$" in and $1\frac{1}{4}$" down from top from right edge of each square. Place hole reinforcements over hole on both sides of each page. Thread jute through page holes and knot ends.

## time-saving tip

### Color-Coordinating Images

Save time coordinating photo colors with papers and create a more dramatic effect by printing color photos in black and white.

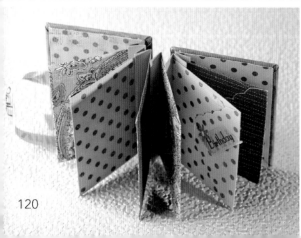

# Joy and Festivity

## Materials

- Acid free adhesives: double-sided tape, glue stick, tacky tape
- Cardstock: light teal
- Chipboard
- Craft scissors
- Envelopes: $2\frac{3}{4}$"x$3\frac{5}{8}$" coordinating colors and patterns (6)
- Gift cards or coupons
- Ribbon: $\frac{5}{8}$" pink (18")
- Scoring tool
- Scrapbook paper: double-sided coordinating colors and patterns (6)

## Instructions

1. **To create covers:** Cut two 4"x3" pieces of chipboard and two 5"x6" pieces of scrapbook paper. Cover chipboard with paper, mitering corners to back side; adhere using glue stick.

2. Center and adhere ribbon horizontally to back side of front cover using double-sided tape, allowing 6" to extend beyond right side.

3. **To create accordion binding:** Cut 8"x4" strip of light teal cardstock; score at $\frac{1}{2}$" intervals across 8" width and fold accordion-style, starting and ending with valley folds. Adhere accordion-fold spine to covers using double-sided tape. *Note:* Be sure to line up the first and last fold of the accordion spine with the edges of the covers. Adhere outside accordion folds together using tacky tape in creases.

4. Cut two $2\frac{3}{4}$"x$3\frac{3}{4}$" pieces of scrapbook paper; adhere to inside of covers using glue stick, overlapping cardstock edges.

5. **To create envelope pages:** Carefully disassemble gift card envelope; use as template to trace and cut six envelopes from double-sided scrapbook paper. Score and fold envelopes; adhere flaps using glue stick.

6. Adhere envelopes into valley folds of accordion spine using double-sided tape. Place coupons or gift cards inside envelopes.

7. Embellish cover as desired. Tie ribbon in a bow.

# Birthday Girl

## Materials

- Acid-free adhesive dispenser
- Cardstock: coordinating colors (3–4)
- Chalk inkpads: coordinating colors (3–4)
- Chipboard
- Cosmetic sponges
- Craft scissors
- Die-cut machine
- Dies: $3\frac{1}{2}$"x$4\frac{1}{8}$" library pocket; $3\frac{1}{8}$"x$4\frac{5}{8}$" tag
- Hole punch: $\frac{1}{4}$"
- Photos: 4"x6" (6)
- Ribbon: $\frac{1}{2}$" coordinating color (12"); $\frac{3}{8}$" grosgrain (36")
- Scoring tool
- Scrapbook paper: coordinating colors and patterns (3–4)

## Instructions

1. **To create covers:** Cut two 6"x$3\frac{1}{2}$" pieces of chipboard. Cover with scrapbook paper, mitering corners to back side; adhere using adhesive dispenser. Cut two $5\frac{3}{4}$"x$3\frac{1}{4}$" pieces of coordinating paper and adhere to back side of chipboard, covering mitered edges. Score and crease front cover 1" from left edge. Embellish cover as desired.

2. **To create pages:** Die-cut six library pockets from paper and assemble. Ink pocket edges using coordinating inkpads and cosmetic sponges.

3. Cut $4\frac{1}{4}$"x$3\frac{1}{4}$" piece of scrapbook paper. Adhere library pocket to each side of rectangle, leaving 1" of left short edge exposed. Repeat two more times to create three sets.

## time-saving tip

### Template Tricks

Save a trip to the scrapbook store by carefully disassembling a purchased library pocket and use it as a template to trace and cut pockets out at home. This also works with other types of pockets and envelopes.

**Above:** Library pockets make perfect sleeves for tucking in tags. **Opposite:** Interactive elements such as these photos cut into simple tag shapes and embellished with coordinating ribbon add interest.

4. Die-cut six tags from cardstock and six tags from photos and adhere back sides together. Ink tag edges. Punch hole in top center of each tag. Cut six 6" pieces of grosgrain ribbon; thread one length through each tag's hole and knot.

5. **To assemble book:** Stack back cover, library pocket pages, and front cover together. Punch two holes through all layers on left edge of book. *Note:* You may need to punch one layer at a time, using the first punched layer as a template for the remaining layers.

6. Thread ½" coordinating ribbon through holes and tie to create binding.

7. Embellish tags and pages as desired; tuck tag into each pocket.

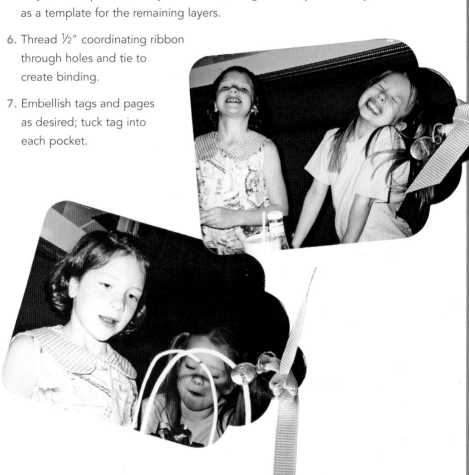

## Personalized Gift

Create this book with unadorned die-cut tags and present to the recipient. He or she can add photos of a celebration with captions after the event for a personalized keepsake.

## About the Author

Roxi Phillips is an award-winning paper and mixed-media artist who has dabbled in a wide variety of crafts throughout her life. Her eclectic style and diversity is shown in her work, from altered art projects to more traditional scrapbooking.

Born and raised in the Pacific Northwest, Roxi developed a love of art in high school and has continued to nurture her talents by taking classes at local colleges and from visiting artists as well as attending conferences and symposiums. She taught preschool for 27 years, with an emphasis on learning through process-oriented art, and shared her passion for encouraging creativity in children with early childhood educators as a teacher-trainer.

Roxi designs paper arts projects using mixed media and scrapbooking techniques for several companies including Krylon® and Tapestry by CR Gibson®. Her work is featured regularly in national magazines such as *Scrapbooking and Beyond*, *PaperCrafts*, and *PaperWorks* and crafting books including *Spray Paint Paper Crafts: Creative Fun with Krylon* (Sterling Publishing ©2006). Roxi is a sought-after instructor of altered arts, book arts, and scrapbooking.

Roxi and her family live in western Tennessee.

## Contributors

Dianne Adams
Ronnie Goff
Marci Lambert
Margaret Lowitzer
Tricia Martin
Pamela Mosby
Jane Mykleby
Barbara Rankin
Robyn Phelan Sharp
Cindy Shipman
Michelle Wilkerson
Candice Windham

## Special Thanks

There are no words to express the gratitude I feel toward my incredible family for their love, patience, and understanding since I received word of the amazing opportunity to write this book. With their support and the talent and incredible dedication of my artist friends, this dream has become a reality. My heartfelt thanks and love to you all.

# METRIC EQUIVALENCY CHARTS

## inches to millimeters and centimeters
(mm-millimeters, cm-centimeters)

| inches | mm | cm | inches | cm | inches | cm |
|---|---|---|---|---|---|---|
| 1/8 | 3 | 0.3 | 9 | 22.9 | 30 | 76.2 |
| 1/4 | 6 | 0.6 | 10 | 25.4 | 31 | 78.7 |
| 1/2 | 13 | 1.3 | 12 | 30.5 | 33 | 83.8 |
| 5/8 | 16 | 1.6 | 13 | 33.0 | 34 | 86.4 |
| 3/4 | 19 | 1.9 | 14 | 35.6 | 35 | 88.9 |
| 7/8 | 22 | 2.2 | 15 | 38.1 | 36 | 91.4 |
| 1 | 25 | 2.5 | 16 | 40.6 | 37 | 94.0 |
| 1 1/4 | 32 | 3.2 | 17 | 43.2 | 38 | 96.5 |
| 1 1/2 | 38 | 3.8 | 18 | 45.7 | 39 | 99.1 |
| 1 3/4 | 44 | 4.4 | 19 | 48.3 | 40 | 101.6 |
| 2 | 51 | 5.1 | 20 | 50.8 | 41 | 104.1 |
| 2 1/2 | 64 | 6.4 | 21 | 53.3 | 42 | 106.7 |
| 3 | 76 | 7.6 | 22 | 55.9 | 43 | 109.2 |
| 3 1/2 | 89 | 8.9 | 23 | 58.4 | 44 | 111.8 |
| 4 | 102 | 10.2 | 24 | 61.0 | 45 | 114.3 |
| 4 1/2 | 114 | 11.4 | 25 | 63.5 | 46 | 116.8 |
| 5 | 127 | 12.7 | 26 | 66.0 | 47 | 119.4 |
| 6 | 152 | 15.2 | 27 | 68.6 | 48 | 121.9 |
| 7 | 178 | 17.8 | 28 | 71.1 | 49 | 124.5 |
| 8 | 203 | 20.3 | 29 | 73.7 | 50 | 127.0 |

## yards to meters

| yards | meters | yards | meters | yards | meters | yards | meters | yards | meters |
|---|---|---|---|---|---|---|---|---|---|
| 1/8 | 0.11 | 2 1/8 | 1.94 | 4 1/8 | 3.77 | 6 1/8 | 5.60 | 8 1/8 | 7.43 |
| 1/4 | 0.23 | 2 1/4 | 2.06 | 4 1/4 | 3.89 | 6 1/4 | 5.72 | 8 1/4 | 7.54 |
| 3/8 | 0.34 | 2 3/8 | 2.17 | 4 3/8 | 4.00 | 6 3/8 | 5.83 | 8 3/8 | 7.66 |
| 1/2 | 0.46 | 2 1/2 | 2.29 | 4 1/2 | 4.11 | 6 1/2 | 5.94 | 8 1/2 | 7.77 |
| 5/8 | 0.57 | 2 5/8 | 2.40 | 4 5/8 | 4.23 | 6 5/8 | 6.06 | 8 5/8 | 7.89 |
| 3/4 | 0.69 | 2 3/4 | 2.51 | 4 3/4 | 4.34 | 6 3/4 | 6.17 | 8 3/4 | 8.00 |
| 7/8 | 0.80 | 2 7/8 | 2.63 | 4 7/8 | 4.46 | 6 7/8 | 6.29 | 8 7/8 | 8.12 |
| 1 | 0.91 | 3 | 2.74 | 5 | 4.57 | 7 | 6.40 | 9 | 8.23 |
| 1 1/8 | 1.03 | 3 1/8 | 2.86 | 5 1/8 | 4.69 | 7 1/8 | 6.52 | 9 1/8 | 8.34 |
| 1 1/4 | 1.14 | 3 1/4 | 2.97 | 5 1/4 | 4.80 | 7 1/4 | 6.63 | 9 1/4 | 8.46 |
| 1 3/8 | 1.26 | 3 3/8 | 3.09 | 5 3/8 | 4.91 | 7 3/8 | 6.74 | 9 3/8 | 8.57 |
| 1 1/2 | 1.37 | 3 1/2 | 3.20 | 5 1/2 | 5.03 | 7 1/2 | 6.86 | 9 1/2 | 8.69 |
| 1 5/8 | 1.49 | 3 5/8 | 3.31 | 5 5/8 | 5.14 | 7 5/8 | 6.97 | 9 5/8 | 8.80 |
| 1 3/4 | 1.60 | 3 3/4 | 3.43 | 5 3/4 | 5.26 | 7 3/4 | 7.09 | 9 3/4 | 8.92 |
| 1 7/8 | 1.71 | 3 7/8 | 3.54 | 5 7/8 | 5.37 | 7 7/8 | 7.20 | 9 7/8 | 9.03 |
| 2 | 1.83 | 4 | 3.66 | 6 | 5.49 | 8 | 7.32 | 10 | 9.14 |

# INDEX